**THIS**

*Tay Poems by Jim Stewart*

THE VOYAGE
OUT PRESS

First published in Great Britain in 2018 by
THE VOYAGE
OUT PRESS

The Voyage Out Press
c/o University of Dundee
School of Humanities
Dundee DD1 4HN

Copyright
© Jim Stewart (Poems)
© Kirstie Behrens (Illustrations)
© Kirsty Gunn ('Foreword')
© Jane Goldman ('About Jim Stewart')
© Alan Hillyer (Author photograph)

Cover design and typesetting by Sian MacFarlane

Printed and bound by Winter and Simpson Print
16 Dunsinane Avenue
Dunsinane Industrial Estate
Dundee DD2 3QT

All rights reserved. No part of this publication may be reproduced
or transmitted in any form or means without prior written permission
of the publisher.

ISBN 978-0-9955123-2-0

*for Ciaran Stewart Flogdell*
*(1991-1996)*

## CONTENTS

**FOREWORD** by Kirsty Gunn   6

**FIELD**

| | |
|---|---|
| Young blackbird | 10 |
| Bindweed | 11 |
| Hive | 12 |
| Plant | 13 |
| Vole | 15 |
| Swifts | 16 |
| Lilac | 17 |
| Cull | 18 |
| Field | 19 |
| Fly | 20 |
| Nest | 21 |
| Earwigs | 23 |
| Oystercatchers | 24 |
| Snowdrops | 25 |
| Rooks | 26 |

**FOREST**

| | |
|---|---|
| Hawah | 28 |
| Blackbird | 29 |
| Six Tentsmuir Riddles | 30 |
| Stream | 32 |
| Tree | 33 |
| Forest | 34 |
| Gall | 35 |
| Cliff | 36 |
| Squirrel | 37 |
| Spider problem | 39 |
| Trees | 40 |
| Berries | 41 |
| Sycamores | 42 |
| Trail | 44 |
| Shield bug | 46 |

## SHORE

| | |
|---|---|
| Gulls | 48 |
| September (ii) | 49 |
| Two dead moles | 50 |
| Balgay Hill | 51 |
| Rook | 52 |
| Ring | 53 |
| Dido | 54 |
| After rain | 56 |
| Old Kiln, Going to Sleep (Two Lyrics for John) | 57 |
| Feather | 58 |
| Cat waking | 59 |
| Night gulls, Dundee | 60 |
| Prayer, interrupted | 61 |
| Shore | 62 |
| Waterfall | 63 |
| Vessel | 64 |
| Bush | 65 |
| White roses | 66 |
| This | 67 |

| | |
|---|---|
| **NOTES & ACKNOWLEDGEMENTS** | 68 |
| **'ABOUT JIM STEWART'** by Jane Goldman | 70 |

## FOREWORD

A horse rolls on the grass and I witness its pleasure. A robin alights on a low branch and gives me its bright eye, 'letting itself be seen', as Jim taught me birds do not often allow. And here's a snail, now, making its way across a sports field; another, smaller, trailing behind it in the dew. A spider dangles from a thread; blackbirds take turns letting each other have their space of song.

Such is THIS, the world opened up to us through the poetry of Jim Stewart. A world intricate with life in all its variety and creativity, an ecosystem fretted with the actions and habits of creatures and seasons that is both everyday and wondrous. And true, while some of the moments listed here are from the selection of work you hold in your hands — this journey of poems that traverse the landscape around the Firth of Tay by one who walked and loved it — some were not. For that is the gift of this artist's work: that it loosens out in us not only in these particular interventions a way of understanding, interpreting, but bestows at the same time upon the reader a means of observation that holds good for all that we might catch in our line of vision. Whether a horse or a worm, this day of rain or another of bright sun... Becoming a way of being, it is, to read Jim's work.

The plant's slow search for form
Bore watching as its stock
Aired these six roots. The vertical
Took a month to find the roof
Then stopped there, bent...         ('Plant')

And look how easy it becomes. To learn how to watch, stand back and wait. We participate in the act of paying attention, is how this work feels to read, witnessing, with the poet, in the natural order of things, a pattern and delight that might usually pertain to the most ornate and highly figured kind of jewelled art.

A complete sense of design is also present in all the poems' formal structures and shapes, that each might match in appearance and sound and image the intricacy of subjects and closely guarded themes. The environment, for this poet, is at one with itself — 'the signs are along the path' — human and animal and vegetal and seasonal all moving in and out of rhyme, seeing and being seen, the subject caught for a minute, as frail and tentative as a creature or plant, as temperature, a season, and all come together as though by chance.

Though the writing, as I know, took much, much longer. 'It can take me years to write a poem', Jim said to me, early on in our friendship, when we started working together to create a writing programme and were talking about our own practice as a way of informing that enterprise. For how can we teach if we don't 'do', as Jim used to say. Or 'make', a word both of us employed from the outset to describe creative process — there in the Greek *poieein* that is at the heart of the word poem. And Jim's poems, yes, took a long time to make.

They might start as a small moment, something glimpsed or seen slow, in long careful contemplation, or they may have had their genesis in a fragment taken from his reading that spoke in turn to something else, an emotion or sense he wanted to attend, capture for a second even, while never presuming to hold it down. And then following that there was the 'processing', as he put it. The thinking through, the reading over. A draft. Another. A line considered... Sometimes that one line would take weeks or more. Then in due course there'd be a printed copy and notes made on that, edits, phrases scored through and others suggested in the margins... 'Oh, yes. Poems take time,' Jim would say. But he always knew he would write them; there were some poems in his mind that had been there from boyhood, he told me. 'I'm still processing these', he said.

I asked Jim about six months or so before his death whether we could have a file of drafts, versions of a poem to use as a teaching resource, that a reader might look on to see exactly how long and with such care it took him to arrive at that final, yet still most flutteringly, fleetingly uncertain, so it seemed, version. In 'Oystercatchers', Jim writes,

> Makeshift, a nest will be let
> and brooded on,
>
> their squealed jitters .
> pooled in yolk,
> in the hot work of embryos...

For is it that a poem is ever finished? Now that Jim has been dead for two years I think more and more that this drafting and redrafting of his was not only part of his modesty as an artist — to shy away from any notion of a shining, completed version and to be moving always, with humility, towards the fashioning of a final idea — but was an expression of how he lived. For to allow the thing time yet to come together on the page, to have it so that it might not ever be quite 'done' but be always in a process of emanating, becoming... This may be a reflection of the man as well as the work.

So then, in this collection of living poems, do we join the poet in the poem, take a part in his sensibility that becomes an ongoing way of thinking, this watching and allowing — a breaking open into meaning as contingent and shifting as the new birds' frail gestures, 'makeshift' and 'brooded on'. The very marks upon the page becoming...*THIS*.

And it's true: who might believe any of this work could ever be finished? That we could close our eyes against it, the minute whirling and turning of animal and human nature with its endlessly renewing mysteries and complications of being and doing, and making and moving that repeats and increases, increases and repeats...

    Only knowing about it, that it's out there, is to be privately engaged, locked as we are in the dark behind our own individual thoughts and selves. Looking, Jim Stewart teaches us in these poems, is another matter.

Kirsty Gunn

## YOUNG BLACKBIRD

The makings of a life
were rounded off this morning
for the young blackbird.

She saw a sky of moving cloud,
the alluring sway of branches
in the window, and went for that.

It was a snap decision.
How could she know what wasn't there
to hurtle into body, mind and soul?

She's warm, but not for long.
Her primaries are flexible.
But her neck has no direction.

The beak dribbles blood
and she's grounded below
the glass that felled her.

Summer will pass; and when it's done,
her skull will present for keeping
its lattice of air.

**BINDWEED**

The funnels, dotted with a few small flies,
seem all the whiter, and the flies more black.

Wherever they flare out, something dies
strangled in the coil of their attack

— maybe a nettle stand that used to rise
against the general wish to cut it back;

or brambles, whose wicked thorns paralyse
flesh with the shock of puncture, and that rack

bare arms with their sprung surprise.
The tender throttling by immac-

ulate blooms might see these off — their guise
of innocence, its unaffected lack

of any guile. So, blessèd be the ties
which binding to reach the light, hijack

other growths. Blessings on all that's wise
for itself alone, on every one-track

nature taking up the slack
unknown to sharpness, for some other prize.

## HIVE

*HEX*
Against attacks of cold or heat
there are no sure spells;
but the thrumming
grubs in their dreams
love this muggy thraldom
where, charmed and mothered
in their wax curbs,
they curl and fatten;
unfold, then break the seals
of their stills
with first impressions.

*DANCE*
They'll trip it among the further blooms,
if the sun's humdrum curve
is rejigged in the steps
of their ceilidh's measures
as trigonometry.
Hungry for the unlearned moves,
they'll summon a star's angle
and, by its numbers,
figure how close they've come
to stripping the willow-herb.

*MIND*
Flicks of their mother's tongue
slurp and mix the nectar with the spit
in their guts' cul-de-sacs;
and to get it they've dredged,
drugged with her pheromone,
the beds of flowers
for licks of that bliss
disgorged in tubs.
Her sweet talk's pledged
a loving-cup from the comb,
once her hungers relax.

**PLANT**

The plant's slow search for form
bore watching as its stock
aired these six roots. The vertical
took a month to find the roof
then stopped there, bent. The others
took the hint; and either pressed the wall
or arabesqued to the side,
feeling for solidity unmet.

Each hair on these tentacles
a foothold, was the start
of sinews, whose mechanic
cause could make such aerial
swerves outreach
for good mould, to put
down weight. Intent, they were
arriving through the volume of the room.

To be strong and to encounter
nothing was the fate
of most, a beckoning space
not to be glibly filled with
all they'd know: in which
they must support themselves somehow
by twists and turns
in the wandering homing cells.
No more the infant corm,
suckling on obscurity or in hock
to the warm dark, their lateral
thought was its own proof,
liminal one way or another,
trembling through draughts to fall
short of ground, to ride
the air, an indefeasible sestet.

To probe the room's ventricles
and test the art
of limitation, the organic
means and ends of radical
love, they wouldn't overreach
themselves; but seek as might suit,
homecoming, fare
afield for the welcome of loam.

Their love kinetic, under
its control, innate
to their trace
of purpose, these feelers willed
a spatial future. Each
squared then with now,
bodying what yearns
to move in their left-right parallels.

It had to come, the hour their long stalk ended.
Roots had found the boundary of need.
Sterile absence forced them to concede.

**VOLE**

Blebs each side of the head —
ripe bramble beads.

A hurry on the path
checks the dyke, the field.

The scurry stops when it squats to nip
a leaf, gripped in frail claws.

Not beneath notice of hawk or human,
it affects indifference

to the wave of fingers
and nibbles the leaf at the edge

of a miniature grace,
a blindsiding of terror.

**SWIFTS**

Haar from the sea's
pleasured sigh,
heavy as houses,
blurred telly dish and chimney stack
and the abbey tower.

Everything was drawn to it,
to where grounded gulls
ran out of gossip,
all things stilled,
the town bell dulled.

No shells tapped at the dyke;
the thrush had lost the snails.
Sometimes in the light
the odd web
shimmied in draughts.

Sick from the thrill of being
yanked along their shrieks,
swifts flung through the fog.

Gulped by its density,
they'd reappear,
shrilling each other down,

fanatically
abandoned to the search
for what sustains
in, and out, of the thick of things.

**LILAC**

No tap root, then. We'd thought
an afternoon and evening not enough
to bare that tail, to gut
its imagined cable. Our hearts sank,
pitted against a dream rod's
wish gripping too deep
– this bush or us.

But spindled underneath
the element it bedded all its life,
no root had lived that way
or had, unreally, sucked such long strength
of being, or ever plumbed
the misgiven ground
of that true lie.

### CULL

The signs are along the path,
every few feet, strewn among gravel:
the half-curves of shattered cups'
broken pinks, their blushed
whorls and roundels, split yellows,
or the dark-striped, with banding
thin or thick. These, which housed
soft bodies for the taking,
are left to ruination. A fragile charm
survives in the smashed colours
— peach orange; green; a browning rose;
impossible shades neither yellow nor pink.
What used to curl inside this light utility
went to the making of song,
to breed more thrushes — flesh
torn from its translucencies to feed
lyrics in the wood.
Unassertive, tender in the grass,
their colours' modesty is everything
it was cracked up to be. A thrush,
fiercely singular, knows only
the glamour of its sound,
nourished on obscure
lesser beauties that cannot fly or sing.

**FIELD**

Maybe healing gets a start
in the ordered natural. The fallow peace,
centre of the present fiction,
was unbroken, unharrowed
twelve months. In its bounds,
ladybirds lagged grassblades with their blood.
Still cocooned
membranes spun a bitter light
into familiar colours.
Earwigs tended eggs and all
hatched to the suffered balm of their enclosure.

True bred, love left the soul
to think about the sedges in the grass
of this walled garden.
Plumbed devotion heard
circling oystercatchers peep,
a scutter in the copse's
hoops and alleys. There, across the fence,
the sudden yellow
darkness must occlude,
as a Brimstone floated off into the wood.

**FLY**

Thunder broke the heat,
and the fat air burst.
This pregnant fly
squat with egg
droned in from the torrent
to muzzle through the rooms
that drew her there
and once in, to the window.

Safe against the rivers
sluicing that glass,
she made her fixed arrangements
in rows of prisms
dabbed on the pane;
and so discharged herself
to die somewhere.

The pouring light,
the light of the rain,
passed through the lenses she had laid,
whose brood would focus soon
its hunger for the odour of decay
no storm in the world
can wash away.

**NEST**

They'd troubled their way into
a traffic cone too heavy for the cat
to topple, its hole
too high; and built inside,

driven by their genes, a cup's
thrift of moss and feather, and of web.
The eye would catch
a flicker, in and out

of the red-and-white geometry,
comings and goings
with pinched grubs
for the craws under that rubber.

One day the commerce ceased.
An old story, of fields
toxic with spray, each gathered meal
deadlier than the last,

made clear
they'd come no more. The cone
lifted, showed five young
with blown-bubblegum crops

that stopped the traffic,
poisoned where they lived
and rendered mulch,
never to fly.
Theirs was the common cup;
but its base uncommonly wide
spread the breadth of the cone,
large dinner plate sized.

The lane once entered,
the signed route kept,
birds had arrived
in their town of children

and couldn't help building out
to what limits exist,
a space made fast
for their homecomings.

The cat flung off
for simpler kills.
The nest's odd architecture
and unseeing idea
settled in a room of the house
where, working blind,
shadows filled
its fixed bowl.

**EARWIGS**

The gathering of dark T-shirts from the line
on a day turned cold
is followed by a shaking out of earwigs
onto the pale floor,

the loss of anywhere to hide
hard on these crevice dwellers
which winter at times in cracks,
bodies flat and wedged

lengthwise into splits
which see out the short days
and frozen nights
huddled in dead heads.

But scattered now from the wrong folds
under strange light
and radiating from where they dropped
lost and single on the lino,

they stop bewildered
on this great space,
useless forks
raised against the shake-out of the days.

**OYSTERCATCHERS**

For long after dark
and before first light
a clamorous pair

of oystercatchers courts
in an echoing circumference
of air and sky.

Anxiously they whoop and wheel
by day, by night. The repetitions mean

that she's in season
and will concede
his ancient cry

that seed should not be lost.
Makeshift, a nest will be let
and brooded on,

their squealed jitters
pooled in yolk,
in the hot work of embryos.

Their keening need
will fold its sound,
bred in the humid shells

they'll make — to shift
and free (peculiar as themselves)
new birds.

**SNOWDROPS**

In the garden's dusk these were
the last lights out,
lambencies that floated
and dwindled in the dark.

When the snow which came for days
reached below the trees
its blank field took
distinction from the blooms.

Depending globes that spotlit
where they sprang from,
even open they shone
nowhere but down.

Winter no time
for the give and take of flies,
they spent their brief glow
searching the ground of themselves.

**ROOKS**

Let go those rooks.

The sky there
between their flights, a figure
of common shape,
is broken,
and through their wings,
the formless air that was
poured around these
bodies.

Grouped by
thought in a quick-
ly constellating
momentary wind,
it's no more than it looks,
and was summoned by the air's
vanishing rigour.

By all means gape
at their fleering token.

The formal principle in things
will not be seen because
this wind that shifted trees
and made the rooks fly
fancy tried its trick
of emulating
in formation.

### HAWAH

She came to the city of souls bearing her branches.
The terror of being was on her. Lost in the crowd,
she clung to her flowers, knowing herself alone.
Their fragrance was comfort, their colour a token of love.

She came to comfort her soul; and bearing its love,
clung to her colours. Knowing the city's terror,
alone in her being she feared the loss of the flowers'
fragrant branches, her token among the crowd.

In the comforting crowd she scented such fragrant souls;
and clung to that knowledge, alone in the city of tokens.
Terror might somehow branch into flowering colour,
bearings not lost if love would come into being.

O city of losses! she came with branches of knowledge.
Bearing her flowers, fragrant she was with love,
her terror of soul (strange comfort, lonely as being)
a clinging token of colour among the crowd.

Bearing her colours, she walked in the terror of knowledge.
Flowers were tokens of loss in this city of beings.
But she clung to their comfort, as if the fragrance alone
could branch into love, there in the soul of the crowd.

Lost in the city's colours, she clung on though knowing
the terror of being without any comfort of flowers;
and crowded by souls; but gallantly bearing her token
branches of fragrance, alone with the coming of love.

**BLACKBIRD**

The blackbird carves a space among the trees.
Blows aren't needed; but it chips the flakes
off rival presences, in territory
hammered out by heavy-chiselled sound.

It isn't always quite so artisan.
Mid-morning, half a dozen flip the fallen
mats of beech leaf, thinning across
the winter grass,

equidistant. Chinking only starts
at morning twilight, or when a slow dusk falls,
foraging not started for the day
or over and done with.

Then comes this vexing of unfilled space
that cannot be shared,
when light and dark throw into doubt
whose area was whose.

For the world turns its back
on former shape in the new air;
and only by a clamorous sculpting's
attacks of sound on memory

do any exact the latent form
of a place's coordinates,
centred as if on them.

**SIX TENTSMUIR RIDDLES**

*II*
I was the last sound heard
by any earbones hidden in my dung.
Time to disappear, breathe out
and not the way you do it, in.
More blood in me than you,
darker muscle, lungs more flat,
I hunt through turbulences, blind,
to eat my fill and feed
the year's child at my teat.

*II*
Fifty feet of dizzy air
don't sicken as I throw myself
from height to reckless height.
Sharp, I split the embryo
of a future tree or sometimes make it grow.
Can't rest. Fidgeting
in roots, on trunks; can't stop.
Can't be at peace. No time.

*III*
I am the water's rhyme
and fluently slip in and out,
unobvious. Fluid all my moves,
it feels as if I am myself this water
and the water's me. My rhyming's full,
not half. I scare the herons;
am unsure of those geese. They swallow
whole: my claws and teeth
rip throats and bellies. Once I'm done,
the birds can have my leavings.

*IV*
For what the herons want is what I want.
The ducks and heavy geese
crave what I crave too.
They are the loch's blank verse.
Only the sound of me
mirrors the depths and surfaces.
Whether I'm downside up
or upside down's no matter.
I rhyme with the sounded water.

V
Which way's down or up
depends what way I face:
I scarper down to the canopy,
or surface to the ground.
Deft as the air itself
which shakes the free seed loose
from any angle of a tree,
my sudden twitch of colour's often seen
flickering sideways.

VI
Now I've reappeared, and breathe again,
the way you do it; now sleep off
the flesh, the guts, the bitten heads.
Resting with the tribe who cry a greeting,
I suckle a year's child;
scat rib and spine, and buried earbones
that hear dead silence,
my muscle's darkened blood
dreaming of shallows and of flood,
of which way's up or down.

**STREAM**

The stream sweetly
deliquescent,
its stone was seen,

the minnow in a water loop,
unlikely under

the lucky shocks.
What this took: slight poise,

a dash here
and there in the onrush.

Pointed to, the discharge,
liquefaction's sign,

shadowed an idea,
the duplicate source.

Drafted letters
in a passing sprint,

its midrash
quick with context,

problematic water
adjusted the enigma of the air.

**TREE**

Inside a silent tree, the looming ring
budges its way per second as the year
presses for acknowledgement of space
to win a half-inch wooden right to life.

Such a grainy slowly growing thing.
Unheard, the bang of pressure is for dear
life itself. It nearly forces grace,
need grown wide through all that minor strife.

The limitation of the bark
is open to the fullest, gladdest greens,
and what seems solid rock is never quite
hard to a heartwood core that both

pushes, from the muteness of its dark
doing and gravely being what it means;
and, gripped by graceful forces, lives to fight
minutely, through the violence of growth.

**FOREST**

Miles off, looking like cliff,
a sodality, columns
strange at this distance,
brinks the sea, blunt trunks
fronting recognition.
Later, slowly approached,
they'll become separate and solid,
and will step apart;
will (upright, distinguished)
concentrate pride,
stiff in their brood of sheaves.
The vernacular of illusion
was momentary. Its gradual
and lateral collapse
sundered its elements
sideways into the simpler things they were,
letting you find a way
among lives you'd want to enter.

Now, spontaneous mosses
and the foggings of lichen
tell tales of the air
the way all webs do.
Aware of a broached space,
you're on more familiar
ground. But further off is a darkness
and it will persist
with its invitation,
the beckoning
to move to a centre
that's never there. And flung, you look back:
the darkness you emerged from
exacted a cost, blood
from bramble-spitted arms,
from skin already dug by grudging twigs.
You'd left what closed behind,
and pushed into obscurity.

### GALL

Tap this, and there tips
from its perfect hole
dust like pollen.
But that is no flower's sperm;
is burrowed powder
left on a surface
for the draught to shift
its quantity of passion.
This ball, the bed of a sleeping egg,
was a stony bud.
The grub dreamed
a move from home
and its hard, unbroken room.
Mining the gall,
it dug a round sky
in which some other wasp,
freed from a far-off barrow,
might flex, to leave
its own soft heap,
the drift of its intent.

**CLIFF**

*WEIGHT*
A mile and a half of air upon the cliff.
That weight to bear, sandstone stands
under a heavy sky.

It takes so long to bend the stone,
but stone will bend. The once hot drops
bedded in its bands
clink and shuffle in the rush,
fresh in the shingle's tricks.

Tons of drifted moths.
Grave gulls, sounding bees
on knapweed and vetch.

Pressure on the rock,
it sinks to the green,
felled by heaven,
by mighty, powdered wings.

*SLIP*
There must have been
a quiet descent of dust
on lost surfaces.

Sift of another colour, a stripe or two,
comes in centuries. Sometimes
seas spill bilge
on land they never fanned before.

A crazy river breaks itself,
shifts the coast, dumps silt,
glints off.

Opals sprayed from sediment
plump in heaps.
Millennial striations slip
the bedrock of the sound.

*SOLID ROCK*
Seen from the pebbled crush
of shells and tangled rope trash:
swallows, the season's trope.

Their nests cooped in friable
Devonian rifts, they thrive
on the edge of a frailty
too slow to stop them cramming flies
in the beaks of their young.

**SQUIRREL**

Ankled in the mulch's grist and pulp,
I climbed a slope,
small under the canopies'
unstirred air; and on the height,
sucked a squirrel-savaged knuckle.

Hearing the squeals from a tangle
where no struggle could save,
I'd stripped back drapes and sticky jock
to cradle that terror; the blood it drew,
spat on stalks of the sudden red grass.

Nearby, the sea sang
of hair-raising purity.

I threw a stone to hear its echo
on the tree trunks.
And threw another in the still pool
to craze the weed and draggle the plants;
and over the chaos, contemplate
the violence that was done upon this water.

**SPIDER PROBLEM**

The body, less weight than area
and light, makes its pitch
trusting the tensile line
hung out to dry, the drop no trouble.
The bottom's too far to care about.
To trip a headlong frailty over the edge
takes for granted a gifted unawareness
blessed where it lands. The vertical's a kind
of flatness, if more awkward. This
is to forget (or never to have known)
how tight is varnish, to have failed to calculate
its proof against purchase by tactile claws.
It is to be suspended on a surface
inviting, but exclusive – frantic, to tap and scrape
at the tip of feeling
that perpendicular, to struggle for long moments,
caressing with each palp's stroke,
each foot's scratch, what doesn't give.

**TREES**

The trees are dreaming of birds,
dreaming their berries are gobbled
by wraiths with not a minute to live,
rendered down to seed, then shat
carelessly through the indifferent air
in a falling feeling coupled
with a splattering sensation who knows where.
They never waken. Torpor guards
their drift to other landscapes, other earth.
Somehow they must sleep themselves to birth,
and all trees have to dream about, is that.

**BERRIES**

*For Kirsty Gunn*

Not to be overlooked
their intense promise
in contrast
to the boughs they furnish
is this thorough red
whose life is not flesh
nor flesh's juice
but the occult seed
passing itself off
richly, here and now.
Their body blush
sticky as blood,
they could be a glutinous
alarm but instead
are agglomerated futures.
The pulp yields
whatever pith or liquor
spirit needs
to be realised
somewhere beyond
the affections of the flesh.

## SYCAMORES
*for Rosalind Flogdell*

First they opened their fat green baby wings,
the air approving, on the side
of this rising flock of seedlings
taking a habitation in its stride.

So many seeds had hatched here in one go.
Lift-off looked inevitable; but
they wouldn't all find space in which to grow.
For any flight path opening, some shut.

Within the week, twin leaves reared
a darker green. Their deep systemic veins
were adult business. When these appeared,
they fielded a fleet of weathervanes,

finger-tested the compass's four ways
to know what side the wind would fly.
It mattered to them: all their wooden days
are a breezy symbiosis till they die.

Air insisted: everything's its own.
Its weight can make the snowdrop droop,
the crocus curve; and bends the will of bone
struggling to resist it or regroup.

All that grows is canted to its lust,
swaying elastically with the sough,
bending back or forward as it must
if the lift is not to snap the bough.

Wind which takes the breath away
does not seek to murder but to shape,
its torque, day by coercive day,
limiting the chances of escape.

The sycamores, too knowing to defy
the onrush of that necessary rhyme,
sank their roots and raised their branches high;
grew forcible; and bided time;

and came at last to the years when they would seed,
when pale propellers turning among the leaf,
torsion in ratio to need,
would hang on their unproved belief.
Wind rose to the occasion too
(an hour of wonder was afoot);
it settled, and conceded to
the resourcefulness of fruit.

Brown blades stiffened to the test
and filled with the truth of trees. Bracts matched
air's motion and, double in their quest
for earth and air, detached.

That was the way their knowhow surfed
the very air, making good
their difference from the breezes they had earthed
by all the airy enterprise of wood.

**TRAIL**

Began at the edge,
moved in a dithering arc.
Then turned back
to the edge.

*

Thicker than thread,
a path fit for use,
it was enough to go on;
and, in some lights,
caught the gleam
reflecting its meaning.

It was an outpouring of need
which, where it lay,
air found and hardened
a shellac scribble
neither aimless nor dogged,
telling itself
not to go there, but here.

*

Starting from the edge, it slowed.
Then its tentative
bend came curving
back to the edge.

*

Over here was a frantic,
decisive fluster
of wavering lines
costing time,
unreadable signatures
and cast-off half-images,
the almost-letters
of nearly-words.
Either what happened
wasn't that much
or what had been done
only seemed like nothing.

\*

Begun at the edge,
it drew to a stop.
A long bend took it
back to the edge.

\*

Around this burst apple,
the glass wreath of traction's
satisfied slide,
where smooth running
left some frizz.

Last night's deposit
shifted the frisson
to where the apple
was knocked by a foot.

And here is the round
where the fruit once was,
its halo of streamers
in the brittle silver
of surrounding want
an encircling of flesh.

\*

It had moved from the edge
to find what it loved.
Once that was found
it returned to the edge.

**SHIELD BUG**

What we do not know, and what we do,
is all the talk among the sons of God.

The caterpillars on October fence posts
judge where in the sun they must pupate.

A shield bug adjusts, new hatched,
to the crash of fire through dawn clouds.

Just as these unthinkingly do and feel,
so we know and do not know of spirit.

SHORE

## GULLS

In this room, gulls' shadows move
Their dark ghosts over the furniture and walls,
Not birds but shades of birds, remote
From the blinding wings that cast them,
Touching with quickly intimate glide
The smoothest of surfaces, the low gloss covers of books,
The mirror's informed eclipse to join
All shape and colour with a gracious passing over.

Gulls tread air, woo all the thermals
Sucking them up. Perched up over sheer
Dizzying drops of rock face, squeal and jabber.
Under the angry thundering they circle
Far away, under the glowering cloud
Glint and teem in a storm of jewels.
Passing over roofs before the sun,
They give their distant shadows to this room,
Subdue all form in the hastening of darkness.

**SEPTEMBER (II)**

Everywhere the spiders blindly weave,
deaf to any threnodies
of headlong flies that can't believe
the summer ends on unseen threads like these.

To see that far ahead is not for flies.
Flies just fly, what more is there to add?
Compound eyes can't pick out spider lies,
or lightness touch the touch a spider had.

The zeroing of their heedless mass
is touching too for its fond
assumption there's no pane of window glass
even there, to fail to fly beyond.

**TWO DEAD MOLES**
*for Peter*

Two dead moles, bloody round the snouts,
baggy and infirm beside the road,
forepaws blessing left and right,
surprised for all time,
their bellies swollen
since the fur gave up the gloss.
Flies nose the breathless bodies,
flit in and out of the mouths.

The yucca silhouetted on the window
in the abandoned night,
its big spikes jag
left and right, their edges
slicing space in sections.
I lie for all time
and mark the inching stars that burrow
eclipsing leaves then swarm
from the further side;
and inhabit the moment's painfulness,
knowing they dicker, from here, in arc and minute;
and there, they hurtle in a burning dream.

**BALGAY HILL**

There once was rhododendron among
graves shadowed by cypress;
and in that rubbish of breakable
twig and bough with the green-black dust,

cradles where blackbird hearts
jumped in their huddled eggs,
speckles gathered at the fat ends,
no batch the same.

Always there was an abandoned clutch.
The yolk could be blown
through careful punctures
and the emptied shells
bedded by the row in sawdust.

Variegation was clear then.
But this was knowledge
exhumed from a bush
and forced to hatch,
a ranking of unincubated
shelled lives, and at the mercy
of a child's fingering.

**ROOK**

He'd climbed a blank horizon with the son
who didn't live with him – to where the snow
lay morsed by rabbits, a bafflingly undone
screed confounding code with bits of crow.
And there they'd seen a rubric in cold blood:
its wings had sliced the snowfield in one
bid to flee remorselessness and go
free beyond the blizzard's purest ton.
Killed from the air, it was dud
feathers lifting lightly with the wind,
fluids leaching into reddish mud.
Here a raptor plummeted and pinned
its prey (not quick enough) against the white
he gazed on as a sorrow stooped to bite.

The snow would vanish and the field be ploughed.
The rook would leave no earthly trace
on cultivated ground. He saw, as clouds
passed over the rise of open space
to visit darkness where no shadow's been,
death had impacted steeply and endowed
a cryptic signature in that place.
Their uphill task would do the gradient proud.
For given the ruptured bird would never preen
primaries again nor ever breed
in a rookery, what else could its blood mean,
fallen in dots-and-dashes from a feed?
The cipher cracked, they read how the bone
wavered and gave, its splintering their own.

**RING**
*for John and Emily*

A ring around a gas giant,
the disc steered by moonlets
commandeers the rubble and the dust.
Further out there are some proper moons.
These too may have a ring's
flummery of rocks unbroken,
*a lusus naturae*
of infants mimicking elders;
and time will pound their sleights
toward some annular poise
solid as but different from the parent.

**DIDO**

For years the sea would surge and foam and race.
She'd feel it in her waters, forced to watch
its slews of spume: the griefs which float
too far to be recovered and that burn
the briny eyes weeping out their salt,
sorrows scuttling sideways like a crab.

Stiff and steady winds would rise to crab
her weeping eyes as though to dry their race
of burning tears and dissipate their salt;
but tears or dryness would not quell her watch
or quench her thirst or make her cease to burn
to know if any undertow would float
her losses home. Her loving grief afloat

would find no harbour. Sideways like the crab
she'd sidle through the running torrent's burn
of outlets in their hectic seaward race,
never to be sidetracked from her watch,
from all these bouts of weeping worth their salt.
And this would be her wage. Immured in salt,

dissipated like the broken flot-
sam's drift to where beachcombers watch,
she'd step among it sideways like the crab,
angular to her family and her race,
on shores of grief, with no more boats to burn.
And as the driftwood beacons rose to burn

the bright bouquets of colour from their salt
and wildly glowing sparkles flew to race
for the depths of midnight sky, figured float-
ing Fishes, Virgin, Water-bearer, Crab
would cancer all her cold and nightly watch,

all those constellations keeping watch
but never witnessing her embers burn,
their own fires long remote. A furtive crab
dithering sideways through the rush of salt,
capsized by the waves then dragged afloat,
her meat would make the hearts of seabirds race.

Sideways like a crab and forced to watch,
her capsized heart would race, her loving burn
the burden of its salt; her longing drift and float.

## AFTER RAIN

Steam drifts off the low roof
after rain. The window's open.
A great bee booms on the glass
its redundant weight.

It shouldn't be able to fly.
Not with that abdomen
slung on its thorax.
Not with that bum.

But there it is. Small wings
a blur, belly
hung on their frailty,
tapping the pane in need

to get to the bushes,
its doomy burr
and delicate lumbering
all bump and growl.

It'll let you guide it by hand.
You only have to steer it
a touch to the left,
take some bad mouthing.

It'll give you the wind of its wings,
its passing draught
without thanks,
blind to your purpose.

*Two lyrics for John*

**OLD KILN**
The old kiln's hiding in the trees.
You have to climb to get there,
can reach it if you care to.

The arches are all limestone under moss.
The ovens have been empty many years.
You have to climb to get there.

It's hiding; turn a corner, there it is.
No smoke, because the ovens all lie cold.
You can reach it if you care to.

The trees are gathered round the cold old kiln.
You'll only find it if you go and search.
You have to climb to get there,
can reach it if you care to.

**GOING TO SLEEP**
Going to sleep in the house you used to live in
isn't like sleeping in the past.
You go to sleep, you wake up,
but now it's not you waking on your own.

Going to sleep in the house you used to sleep in
isn't the same as living in the past.
You go to sleep, you wake up,
but now you're dreaming the dreams of two.

Going to sleep in the house you used to dream in
isn't the same as dreaming in the past.
You go to sleep, you wake up,
new dreams are here, the daylight's different.

**FEATHER**

Some breast lost this.

The need passed,
it hinders no flight,
means no heat loss.
Plenty others
keep out the cold,
or spread the flush
of bird blood.

Its fix on flesh
wrong at the root,
too odd to hang long,
loosening wind
undid the tie;
or while the pecked
ground
gave grist for a crop.

Shaft and barb idle
in a corner's draught
not light like the air,
nor riding a wind,
which plucks and shifts
in the old way.

**CAT WAKING**

She unfolds herself, slightly deranged,
from the sleep of the just. Outside the room,
November is bare branched, damp; its cold
increasingly has designs
on birds tormenting the twigs
for whatever's there.

The heating off all night, the temperature drop
felt through her fur
(a mist inside the window,
drizzled by the cold,
will vanish when the heat's back on)

prints the panes with her lung water,
breath of her nostrils. What is in it
is dreams. They fogged the glass
with her fear of other cats, shrilling of birds,
noises demanding explanation,
dog-bark streets off; the grip in her gut
of feeding long delayed.

She has stretched each muscle. Each whisker
trembles in the light. She forgets
the traumas of rest. Warmth pays
its visit to the room. On the window,
the moisture of her visions starts to clear.

**NIGHT GULLS, DUNDEE**

Given that I know there are no ghosts
and that the only phantom is my fear,
what would cause this shudder isn't clear
as the night gulls glide through Dundee in their hosts.

Maybe it's because they always scream
but now are quiet, appearing from a dark
I didn't know contained them; stark
and white and half remembered from a dream.

The night is theirs not mine. The vacant street
walked by all the generations dead
is flown by birds that, having lost their dread,
rip the precinct's bin bags for their meat.

Maybe these are the wraiths of gulls long gone,
their suddenness what gave this mild alarm,
focussed and impervious to harm,
stomachs empty hours before the dawn.

Their silent spirits close to mine, I can't
think what made me start like this. They fly
in search of lost, abandoned food; and I
haunt their streets, untimely, revenant.

**PRAYER, INTERRUPTED**

That the word might make sense,
and explain itself,
that impulse might be good,

skewed by pungent
elderflowers' tang
drawing flies to the must.

That service live in all exchanges,
that laughter and mercy join
their lucid strengths,

flung by the heartbreak
that is honeysuckle
whose courtship is urgent
and its days brief

and which is crossed by thrush call
to the listening trees,
with its loud response
from over there.

## SHORE

*II*
This shore is where the water and the land
compose their strip of shifting compromise.
Dunes grow semi-stable; and their sand

faces down the tides' untiring tries
to force a shapelessness upon each grain
and stop it ever rounding where it lies.

Marram grass's roots defy that rain
of breakers pouring down and help immure
in density the form they stand to gain,

bedded and compacted, to secure
something's retrieval from a grudging sea,
even something permanent and sure.

*II*
The secret water hides its storied
source. And so the seabirds eye the weed
it squanders, and harass the worried

crabs that scutter into range of need.
The current, always truculent and blind,
dragged by the moon, its longings feed

on sunken definitions, uninclined
to let emerge whatever doesn't flow
in strict assimilation to its mind,

dissolving by immersion. So
no edge survives or any sharpness not
blunted by its determined undertow.

**WATERFALL**

This is a quick and easy passage down;
and freely overgoverned by its fall
into the water where you cannot drown,

it gushes from the marshes' shallow brown
a purity that's hardly stained at all.
This is a quick and easy passage down

of tribute rashly pouring from the crown
homage to itself but past recall
into the water where you cannot drown.

Glossing more as verb than passive noun
the rushing of its gerunds in control,
this is a quick and easy passage down.

So long as marginalia expound
this rhetoric glissading down its wall
into the water where you cannot drown

and nuance isn't free to play around
with surplus syllables at large or small,
this is a quick and easy passage down,
into the water where you cannot drown.

**VESSEL**

*LIGHT*
boat ticking over the deep,
twitch on that broadest of backs,
no mark visible from the miles above
or miles under the abyss – midge,
straw-fleck adrift in its wide sky,
why do you do what you do and point
your minor ingenuity
and small magnificence
at an overwhelming light
too great for you to look at
which will quietly absorb you
if and when you arrive?

*WRATH*
anger is reasonable and righteous
but cross the line and something more than this
awaits, or worse, comes seeking.
It will not bargain or listen to a plea
made too late; will take the shape
of a northern threat, its rigging of bolts
the nerves of light in the first spit
of an equatorial downpour.
Sail on, storm-blind. As you wish.
Keep your course, rebellious heart.
It will not save you.

*MERCY*
finally, after great foolishness,
the advent of calm
that follows the idiot risks
and the long-unanswered prayer,
with only these little splashes to the side
to indicate motion. Stillness on the deep;
move, boat. It hardly matters where.
Darkness full upon the broken waters,
let creation begin.

Paul's 'Epistle to the Romans' (chs.8-9) is a source for his famous meditation on Christian and non-Christian destinies. The proems to Genesis chapter one and (eventually) to the Fourth Gospel would prove to be, in time, the frame for all such meditations, including influential reflections by Augustine and Calvin.

## BUSH

The way this bush has gathered in the darkness.
The way it deepened, thinking of itself.
The way this darkness deepened in the bushes
and how the gathering darkness hid itself.

The way the kinds of darkness were distinguished.
The way that green dark differed from dark green.
The way the different darknesses foregathered
and how the darker differences emerged.

The fact this bush will vanish into darkness.
The fact the dark is welcoming the bush.
The fact that bush and dark are not distinguished.
The fact the bush is gathered by the dark.

**WHITE ROSES**

The breeze blew strong all day.
Smoke from the garden's pile
of nettles and dried mats of grass
was proud and seething, creamy thick.

Sprinklers up the field
flung rainbows while they wound
tense on their hoses. Their vapour's sift
shot where the smoke blew bright;

but no eye told apart
that fume from spray
or knew, by only looking,
the given water, the fire's thanks.

To gloss those differences
downwind of the white roses
was to know blessing.

**THIS**

is this, and this only:
how the kestrel knows
air, not as
the owl knows it, or the wasp.

What's what
is this: the bat
flying near blind
in the wake of its sound.

And also this:
a slight
movement in the grass,
caught in its history.

## NOTES

The following poems were first published in:
'Bindweed', *NWD* 3 (2008)
'Hive', *Gutter* 5 (2011)
'Berries', *Gutter* 2 (2010)
'Cull', *Dundee Writes* 6 (2013)
'Fly', *Northwords Now* 18 (2011)
'Gulls', *Seagate* II (1984)
'Earwigs', *NWD* 5 (2010)
'Spider Problem', *Dundee Writes* 8 (2017)
'Balgay Hill', *NWS* 29 (2011)
'Rook', *riverrun* 4 (2003)
'Night Gulls, Dundee', *Whaleback City* edited by Andy Jackson and W. N. Herbert (Dundee University Press, 2013)
'Waterfall', *The Red Wheelbarrow* 6 (2001)
'Bush', *NWD* 1 (2006)
'Feather', *Working With Words* (Tayside Healthcare Arts Trust, 2010)
'Vessel', *The Voyage Out* edited by Kirsty Gunn and Gail Low (The Voyage Out Press, 2016)

## ACKNOWLEDGEMENTS

With thanks and love to the following for their help in putting this collection together:

Reinhard Behrens
Geoff Flogdell
Marilla Flogdell
Rosalind Flogdell
Jane Goldman
Kirsty Gunn
Susan Haigh
Alan Hillyer
Adam Learmonth
Gail Low
Lynsey Macready
Lindsay Macgregor
Edward Small
John Stewart
Peter Stewart
Emily Stewart-Rayner

We are also grateful to all who have donated so generously to make the publishing of this title possible.

All design work and illustrations have been gifted.

Illustrations are by Kirstie Behrens, an artist who lives and works in Pittenweem, Fife. A final year fine art student at DJCAD, University of Dundee, she has been making etchings as a means of expressing her interest in natural form, particularly trees and mountain scenes. More of her work can be seen at https://www.kirstiebehrens.co.uk/

Design and typesetting are by Sian MacFarlane, a Newport-on-Tay graphic designer and graduate of DJCAD now based at Glasgow. More of her work can be seen at: https://www.sianmacfarlane.org

## ABOUT JIM STEWART

James Clark Quinn Stewart, born in 1952 to a working class family in a cold tap and outside toilet dwelling on the Lochee Road, Dundee, barely survived a near-fatal bronchial illness in early infancy. He and his younger sister, Ros, were then brought up by their single mother, a devout Jehovah's Witness, in a semi-detached new build on Gourdie Terrace, a few miles to the west. Sometimes at odds with the evangelical church that shaped family life, Jim was devout all of his life, and highly learned in theology. Called after a clergyman admired by his mother, the sight from the bus of his own name in big black letters on a local church front would make him smile. The ten-year-old Jim ran home one day with his sister from a visit to the public baths, both of them full of wonder after watching a burly older man with a wooden leg swim sleek as a seal through the water, and then stand hearty in the showers close by them. A full decade passed before their mother let them know that this marvellous aquatic creature had been their grandfather. It was their only encounter with him.

Jim left Harris Academy, Dundee, at fifteen somewhat disillusioned by school life, to work in a local supermarket. A year later the family moved to Brechin where Jim took various jobs, as sign writer, assistant in an antique shop, and window cleaner. He moved to Arbroath when he was twenty-one, married Susan and had a son, Sean (who in 2014 predeceased him). He worked as a proofreader for the local newspaper, *The Arbroath Guide*, became a regular reviewer for the music page, and progressed to news reporter. He was sacked after he refused to doorstep a family caught up in a divorce scandal.

Jim moved back to Dundee when he and Susan divorced, and went to college to qualify for entrance to university. He married Bridget, with whom he had two sons: Peter and John. Family always important to him, he was also a father figure to Marilla Flogdell, his niece. In 1984 Jim graduated from the University of Dundee with a first-class honours degree in English Literature. He undertook a PhD at the University of Edinburgh, researching Virginia Woolf, and gained his doctorate in 1990. From 1987 until his death Jim was employed at the University of Dundee, for the most part on numerous precarious short-term teaching contracts, and occasional research contracts (on a W. H. Auden Concordance, and later the Cambridge University Press Edition of Virginia Woolf). Often obliged to fall back on window-cleaning and proof-reading in employment gaps, Jim was nevertheless an indefatigable and inspirational teacher, of formidable intellect, to generations of admiring students, and a loyal and stalwart colleague. He became a Woolf scholar of considerable international repute, and in 2014 he was made a permanent staff member at Dundee, following the success of the MLitt in Writing Practice and Study.

    Jim wrote poetry from childhood onwards, almost continuously, and published in numerous magazines over the years (the earliest in 1966). He became a major force in the development of the University of Dundee's Creative Writing curriculum, in which he found his true academic element. As well as lyric poetry, he wrote the libretto for the opera *Flora and the Prince*, composed by Graham Robb, and in 2012 travelled to New York to see it staged at Carnegie Hall. For many years Jim had been planning a collection of his own poetry, to be called ('plain and simple') *THIS*. He was beginning to see the volume to fruition just as he became fatally ill with cancer. He died on 24th June 2016. There was only one event in Jim's rich and sometimes turbulent life that caused him ever to doubt his own powerful calling as a poet, and that was the untimely death of his five-year-old nephew. It was his wish to dedicate *THIS* to the memory of Ciaran Stewart Flogdell.

Jane Goldman